SPOT

BACKYARD BIRDS

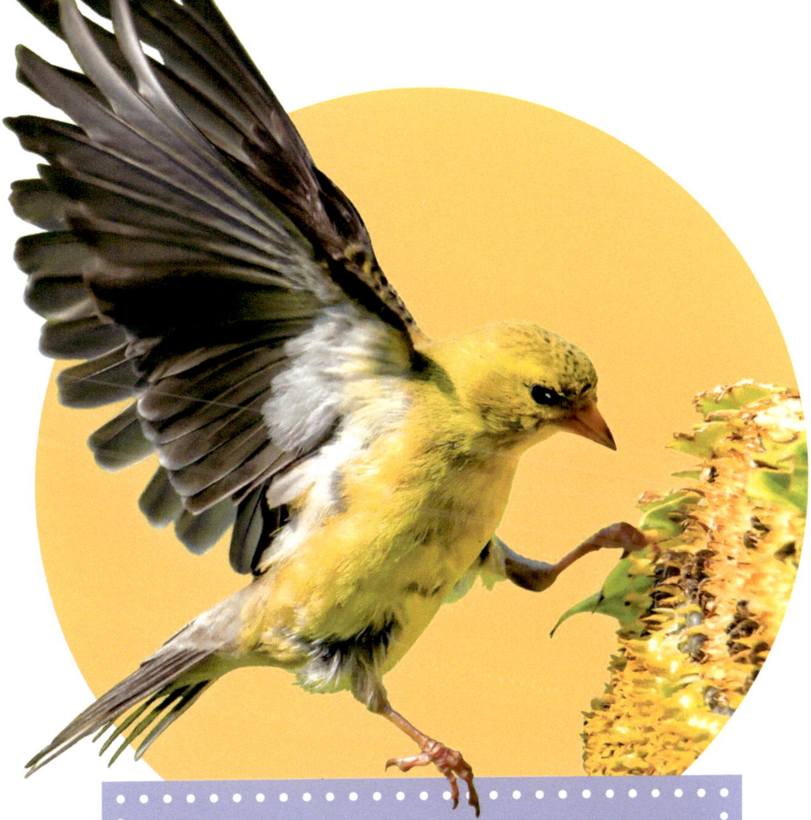

GOLDFINCHES

by Anastasia Suen

head

seeds

Look for these words and pictures as you read.

nest

bath

Have you seen this bird?
It is a goldfinch.
This bird has yellow feathers.

head

Their wings are black and white. Males have a black spot on their head.

Colors change in the winter.
Yellow feathers fall out.
Brown ones grow in.

These birds do not like bugs.
They mostly eat seeds.

nest

Mom builds a nest in a tree.
An old spiderweb holds it tight.
Six eggs rest inside.

Splish! Splash!
It's time for a bath.
These birds love water.
bath

A goldfinch is a backyard bird.
Have you seen it?

head

seeds

Did you find?

nest

bath

Spot is published by Amicus Learning, an imprint of Amicus
P.O. Box 227, Mankato, MN 56002
www.amicuspublishing.us

Library of Congress Cataloging-in-Publication Data
Names: Suen, Anastasia author
Title: Goldfinches / by Anastasia Suen.
Description: Mankato, MN : Amicus Learning, [2026] | Series: Spot backyard birds | Audience: Ages 4-7 | Audience: Grades K-1 | Summary: "Goldfinches are small yellow birds found across North America. This search-and-find book reinforces new vocabulary words with simple facts and compelling photographs to teach kindergarten and first grade readers about backyard birds"— Provided by publisher.
Identifiers: LCCN 2025010592 (print) | LCCN 2025010593 (ebook) | ISBN 9798892008327 library binding | ISBN 9798892008983 paperback | ISBN 9798892009645 ebook
Subjects: LCSH: Goldfinches
Classification: LCC QL696.P246 S84 2026 (print) | LCC QL696.P246 (ebook) | DDC 598.8/85—dc23/eng/20250717
LC record available at https://lccn.loc.gov/2025010592
LC ebook record available at https://lccn.loc.gov/2025010593

Printed in United States of America

Ana Brauer, editor
Deb Miner, series designer
Sara Hood, book designer and photo researcher

Photos by Dreamstime/Noah Strycker, 2, 10–11, 15; Getty Images/Beata Whitehead, 3, Dennis Govoni, 1, photo by Victoria Ross, 6–7, Vicki Jauron, Babylon and Beyond Photography, 2, 4–5, 15; Shutterstock/Arianne N. James, cover, Melody Mellinger, 2, 12–13, 15, Mircea Costina, 2, 8–9, 15, Tony Campbell, 14